City Trucks

Julie Murray

abdobooks.com

Published by Abdo Kids, a division of ABDO, P.O. Box 398166, Minneapolis, Minnesota 55439. Copyright © 2024 by Abdo Consulting Group, Inc. International copyrights reserved in all countries. No part of this book may be reproduced in any form without written permission from the publisher. Abdo Kids Junior™ is a trademark and logo of Abdo Kids.

Printed in the United States of America, North Mankato, Minnesota.

052023

092023

THIS BOOK CONTAINS RECYCLED MATERIALS

Photo Credits: Alamy, Getty Images, Shutterstock

Production Contributors: Teddy Borth, Jennie Forsberg, Grace Hansen

Design Contributors: Candice Keimig, Pakou Moua

Library of Congress Control Number: 2022946714

Publisher's Cataloging-in-Publication Data

Names: Murray, Julie, author.

Title: City trucks / by Julie Murray

Description: Minneapolis, Minnesota : Abdo Kids, 2024 | Series: Trucks at work | Includes online resources and index.

Identifiers: ISBN 9781098266110 (lib. bdg.) | ISBN 9781098266813 (ebook) | ISBN 9781098267162 (Read-to-me ebook)

Subjects: LCSH: Trucks--Juvenile literature. | Vehicles--Juvenile literature. | City transit--Juvenile literature.

Classification: DDC 388.32--dc23

Table of Contents

City Trucks. 4

More City Trucks. . . .22

Glossary. 23

Index 24

Abdo Kids Code. 24

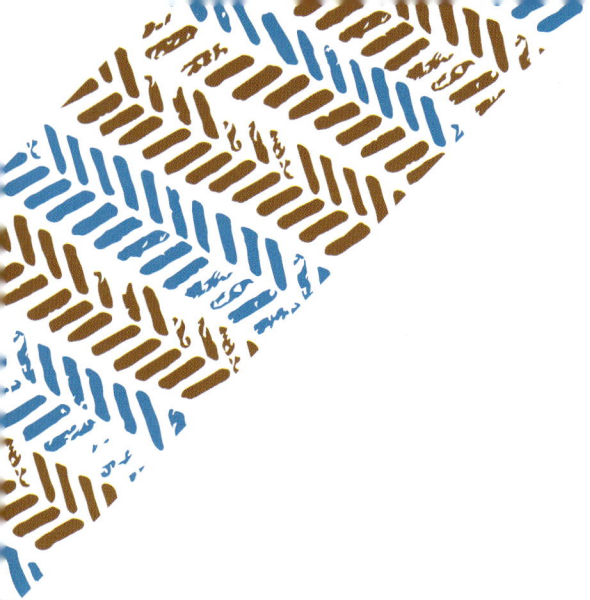

City Trucks

City trucks help keep cities running smoothly!

A mail truck brings the mail.

A mail carrier drives it.

A garbage truck is big!

The arm lifts the can.

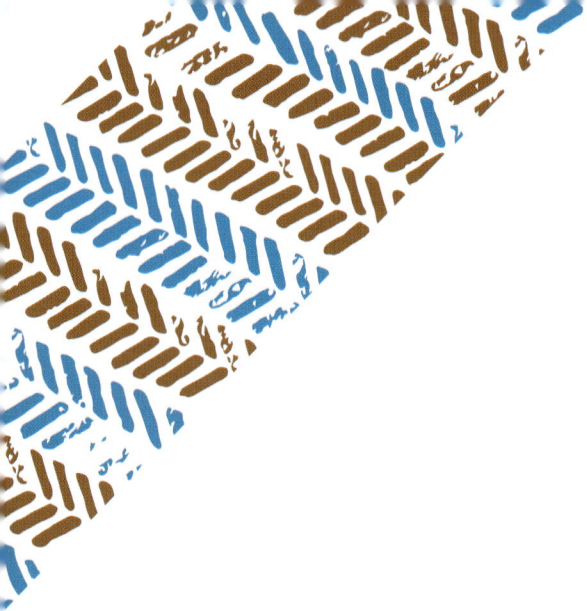

Al drives a water truck. He waters the street flowers.

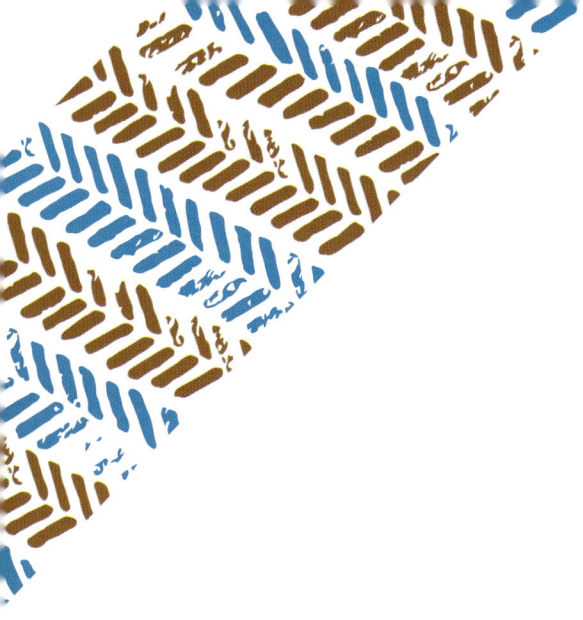

A **recycling** truck comes to Val's house once a week.

13

A bucket truck lifts Ian.

He fixes the power line.

Pam drives a snowplow.

She makes the roads safe.

A **freight** truck moves goods. Sam helps unload.

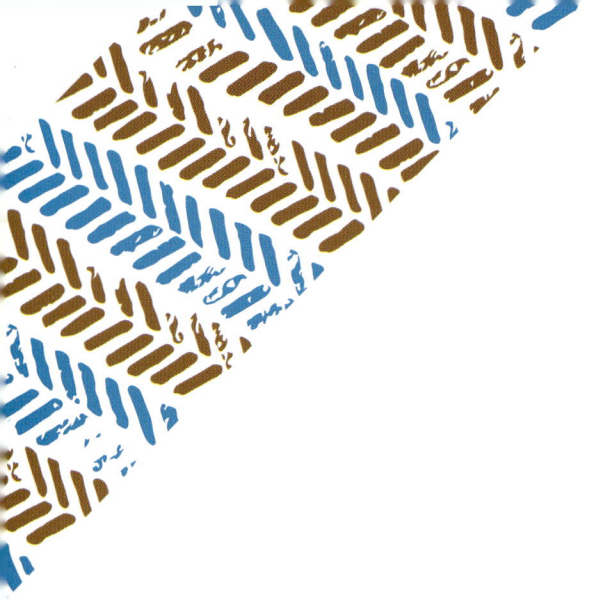

What trucks do you see in your city?

More City Trucks

deicing truck

street cleaner

striping truck

tow truck

Glossary

freight
goods shipped by boat, plane, train, or truck.

recycling
the activity of processing things so that they can be used again.

Index

bucket truck 14

freight truck 18

garbage truck 8

mail truck 6

recycling truck 12

snowplow 16

water truck 10

Visit **abdokids.com** to access crafts, games, videos, and more!

Use Abdo Kids code **TCK6110** or scan this QR code!